A DUBIOUS LEGACY

When you are a single girl, carefree and not quite twenty, you think a lot about love and sex and marriage. You think about your own love life, and about other people's marriages – especially if the husband is tall, amusing, and married to a perfectly horrible woman, who chooses to spend most of her time alone in bed.

Antonia and Barbara, visiting Henry and Margaret for the first time, think their marriage is peculiar and mysterious. Why does Margaret stay in bed all the time? Why is she so nasty to Henry? Why is Henry so forgiving? Antonia and Barbara are soon married, and they and their husbands are regular visitors to Henry's farmhouse in the country. And as the years pass, their children come, and they in turn bring their own children.

Very few people have uncomplicated lives, and Henry and his friends all have little secrets to tell – if they choose to. But some secrets are best left untold, and some mysteries are best left unexplained. As the English proverb says, 'Let sleeping dogs lie.'

OXFORD BOOKWORMS LIBRARY
Human Interest

A Dubious Legacy

Stage 4 (1400 headwords)

Series Editor: Jennifer Bassett
Founder Editor: Tricia Hedge
Activities Editors: Jennifer Bassett and Christine Lindop

MARY WESLEY

A Dubious Legacy

Retold by
Rosalie Kerr

Illustrated by
Gary Wing

OXFORD UNIVERSITY PRESS

OXFORD
UNIVERSITY PRESS

Great Clarendon Street, Oxford OX2 6DP

Oxford New York
Auckland Bangkok Buenos Aires Cape Town Chennai
Dar es Salaam Delhi Hong Kong Istanbul Karachi Kolkata
Kuala Lumpur Madrid Melbourne Mexico City Mumbai Nairobi
São Paulo Shanghai Taipei Tokyo Toronto

Oxford and Oxford English are registered trade marks
of Oxford University Press in the UK and in certain other countries

ISBN 0 19 423057 0

Original edition Copyright © 1992 by Mary Wesley
This simplified edition © Oxford University Press 2003
First published in the Oxford Bookworms Library 2003

Database right Oxford University Press (maker)

Printed in Spain by Unigraf s.l.

CONTENTS

PEOPLE IN THIS STORY

Henry Tillotson
Margaret Tillotson, *his wife*
Trask, *works for Henry on the farm*
Pilar, *a refugee from Spain*
Ebro, *Pilar's son*

John
Jonathan } *the 'two Jonathans', friends of Henry's*

Hector
Calypso } *a married couple, friends of Henry's*

Peter Bullivant
Maisie Bullivant } *a married couple, friends of Henry's*

James Martineau
Barbara, *his girlfriend, later his wife*
Hilaria, *Barbara's daughter*
Eliza, *Hilaria's daughter, and Barbara's granddaughter*

Matthew Stephenson
Antonia, *his girlfriend, later his wife*
Susie
Clio } *Antonia's daughters*
Katie, *Clio's daughter, and Antonia's granddaughter*

Basil, *Margaret Tillotson's brother*

1
MARGARET COMES TO COTTESHAW

'I thought you said you had a car.'

The horse at the front of the cart turned its head at the sound of the woman's voice. She was tall, with red-gold hair and white skin. Her mouth was painted a bright red, and she stared at the horse with green eyes.

The horse stared back at the woman and then, recognizing the man behind her, lifted its head and stepped forward. The woman moved back quickly. 'How horrible,' she said.

The man put his hand on the horse's neck. 'Hello, Nellie, you dear old thing,' he said. He turned to the woman. 'Nellie will take us home in this cart, and our luggage will come in the other cart.'

'Carts? You said you had a car. A Bentley, you said.'

'I have. It was my father's.'

'Then why isn't it here to meet us?'

'Because it's a very expensive car to drive, and we can't use it in wartime. Come on, jump in the cart.'

'No.'

'Why didn't you tell me you were afraid of horses?'

'I'm not. I don't *like* them.' Margaret Tillotson stared at her husband.

The man who had put the luggage on the second cart came

towards them. 'Everything all right, Henry?' he asked.

He was a small man, in an open-necked shirt and grey trousers. He was a servant, Margaret supposed, but he called Henry 'Henry', not 'Mr Tillotson'.

'My wife was expecting the Bentley,' said Henry Tillotson, smiling. He turned to Margaret. 'This is Trask,' he said. 'We depend on Trask.'

Trask smiled. 'Pleased to meet you.'

Margaret moved her red lips a little, showing excellent teeth, but said nothing.

Trask, looking at Henry, said, 'What about the station taxi? It'll be back in a minute.'

'Good idea,' said Henry cheerfully. 'And how is everything?' he asked Trask. 'How are Pilar and Ebro?'

'They're fine.'

'Pilar is the Spanish girl I told you about,' Henry told his wife. 'Ebro is her son. He must be about four now.'

'Nearly six,' said Trask.

'Pilar is your servant,' said Margaret.

'Not exactly a servant, she's a refugee,' Henry said.

'But she cleans the house for you.'

'Well, yes, but nobody asks her to.'

'*I* shall,' said Margaret.

When the taxi came, Henry held the door open, Margaret got in, and Henry closed it. Alone on the seat, Margaret said, 'But aren't you—?'

'No, I'm driving Nellie,' Henry said.

As the carts drove away and the taxi followed slowly

behind them, Margaret stared at Henry's back in the cart, and her mouth narrowed to a thin red line. She made no reply to any of the taxi-driver's friendly conversation.

The little road climbed into some hills, and then went down into a valley, passing fields full of sheep, and woods where the leaves were turning red and gold.

'It's pretty countryside round here,' the driver said. 'And there's the house. Cotteshaw. Is it as grand as you expected? I think it's a nice house. Not too big and not too small.'

It was a lovely old house, built of light brown stone, and with walls covered in climbing roses. Margaret noted that its doors and windows needed painting, and saw also that a young woman stood smiling on the front steps.

She was short and square, with black hair and small black eyes. The child holding her hand looked just like her. They were not good-looking, but their happiness at seeing Henry lit their faces with beauty.

'Pilar!' Henry cried, 'and Ebro!' He hugged them both. Two dogs ran out and jumped excitedly around him. 'It's good to be home,' he said. 'Wonderful.'

'Your wife?' said Pilar.

'In the taxi,' said Henry, smiling. 'Come and meet her.' He opened the taxi door. 'Did you enjoy the drive?'

Margaret Tillotson stepped out of the car.

'She *hit* him?' the landlord of the village pub said to Trask the next day. 'Whatever for?'

'Wasn't for love.' Trask drank some beer. 'She seemed kind

3

Margaret Tillotson stepped out of the car.

of annoyed,' he said. 'She hit the horse on the nose with her bag, and then she hit Henry right in the eye.'

'And what happened next?'

'Pilar took her upstairs, to show her the bedrooms. Madam chose the best one, and made Pilar unpack her luggage. After that it was, "do this, do that, light the fire, bring me hot soup." Then she went to bed. And she's still there. In bed.'

'Is she ill?' said the landlord. He refilled Trask's glass.

'No. Pilar says she isn't.'

'And Henry? What did he do?'

'He went out walking with his dogs. He was out most of the night, Pilar says.'

The landlord gave Trask a worried look. 'Whatever shall we say to Henry when he comes in for his beer?' he said.

'He won't be in,' said Trask. 'I've just taken him to the station. He's gone back to the war.'

—◇—

Henry Tillotson watched Trask drive the cart away from the station. Then he left his bag at the station office, and walked away, over the fields, through a wood, and into the garden of a small house. There was a ladder against one of the trees, and he stopped by it and looked up.

'Too busy with his new wife to come and see his boring old friends,' said a voice among the leaves.

'I'm here. I've come,' Henry said. He shook the ladder.

'Don't do that. It's dangerous. I might fall.'

'What are you doing up a tree, anyway?' Henry said.

'Picking apples, my dear. It's the war, you know. John says

5

we have to make good use of every apple we grow.' He came down the ladder. 'Oh, dear boy, it's good to see you!' He kissed Henry warmly, studying his face. 'Shall we go to the house and find John? He's making cakes in the kitchen.'

Henry said, 'Yes, Jonathan, all right, let's do that.'

They walked in silence at first, then Jonathan said, 'We heard, of course, and then you wrote, but you didn't . . .'

Henry avoided this unspoken question, and said quickly, 'So you're John and Jonathan now? Not both Jonathan, which is the name you were both given.'

'Yes. I'm older than John, so I keep the name, although we both like it.' Then he called, 'Look who I've found!' as they entered a stone-floored kitchen.

'Just in time for tea!' said a tall, red-haired man. 'And my cakes are just ready. Oh, dear boy! You didn't forget us!'

For a moment they all stood smiling at each other. Then John said, 'Sit down and tell us everything. We want to hear all about it. It's something so exciting in our boring lives!'

Henry said, 'Those cakes smell delicious.' He paused. 'There's nothing to tell.'

He watched as the two men fetched cups, cut cakes, and made tea. The two Jonathans, as they were often called, had been his friends since childhood. Now they seemed worried, and Henry sat, wondering and waiting.

There was some talk about the neighbours, and the war, then John asked, 'Will you stay the night?'

'I have to catch the late train. I go to France tomorrow.'

'Your mother,' said Jonathan, 'was very fond of France.'

'But not so fond of the French,' said John.

Why are they talking about my mother? Henry wondered. 'My mother has been dead a long time,' he said.

'And your dear father,' said John. 'Our godfather, God rest him. He was so kind to the two little Jonathans.'

'I asked him once,' said Henry, cutting another piece of cake, 'if you were his brother's children. But he said no.'

'We never knew who our fathers were,' said Jonathan. 'But your father paid for us to go to school, and everything. The dear man. He did so many acts of kindness in his life.'

Henry banged his hand down on the table, knocking a plate to the stone floor, where it broke. 'I'd like to break another,' he said angrily.

'Please do,' John said. 'Let yourself be angry. It's supposed to be good for you.' He seemed worried, a little ashamed.

These two know something, Henry thought. It's making them feel uncomfortable. There's something strange here.

'So you've come to tell us all about your marriage?' said Jonathan bravely.

Henry, who had come to do exactly that, said, 'No. No, I haven't.' But later, as they walked with him to the station, he asked them, 'Will you go and see my wife? Get to know her? See what you can do?'

They said of course they would. There was nothing they would enjoy more.

———◇———

As they walked home in the dark, Jonathan said, 'It's gone wrong this time, hasn't it?'

'It was when we talked about acts of kindness. It made him angry. That's when he banged the table.'

'And yet, with Pilar . . .'

'But his father saw Pilar, found her himself, offered her a home, and so on,' said John. 'This isn't the same thing; this was an act of kindness that somebody *else* had to do.'

'But asking him to ask Henry seemed a good idea.'

'Yes. At the time.'

Jonathan started to laugh. 'I can't wait to meet her. It's awful to laugh. Did you see the marks where she hit him?'

John laughed too. 'Let's visit her as soon as we can!'

'Oh dear! Why did we get involved in this?' said Jonathan.

'A bit late to ask that now,' said his friend.

—◇◇◇—

It was years before the Jonathans spoke about their visits to Margaret. They told Calypso, who was an old friend of Henry's, and who could keep a secret.

On that first visit, they said to Calypso, they put on suits and carried roses. Margaret sat in her bed.

They found her beautiful, but at first conversation was difficult. Then they discovered that she wanted to change the way her room looked. They offered to help, telling her they were interested in things like that. She told them that her ex-husband was the same as them. He was 'queer', not a real man. 'She wanted to hurt us,' they told Calypso. Still, they tried to help her. They had promised Henry that they would.

They brought in mirrors and chairs, found paint and paper for her room. They enjoyed doing it, and it helped Henry.

Margaret paid for nothing. She had money but she wouldn't buy anything except her own clothes.

At first they expected her to get out of bed, to take an interest in Cotteshaw, to behave like Henry's wife. Their hopes died on that first visit. Margaret made it clear that there would never be any question of love, or sex, or friendship. Henry was caught in a terrible trap.

'We blamed ourselves for it all,' Jonathan told Calypso, and she saw that he was crying.

'But you did what Henry asked you to,' she said. 'And over the years, Margaret has given you a lot of amusement.'

They had to agree. Margaret's stories delighted them. She was a terrible liar. One week she had been born in Beirut, the next in Brighton. One day she was born rich, the next day she was so poor that she had to work as a servant.

It was all much more interesting than the truth, they told Calypso. They were almost sure that she had actually been a hairdresser in a Cairo hotel.

When they had gone, Calypso wondered why they had not been brave enough to tell her of the part they had played in Henry's marriage. Then, since other people's secrets did not interest her, she forgot about it.

2
Invitation to Cotteshaw

James Martineau and Matthew Stephenson, meeting in a London street, discovered that they had both been invited to Cotteshaw for the coming weekend.

'Henry suggested that I should bring a girl,' Matthew said. 'So I've asked Antonia. Are you taking a girl?'

'I'm thinking of asking Barbara,' James said.

'Excellent. They're great friends, so that'll be nice for Antonia. It should be a good weekend, in fact. Henry's parents used to give wonderful dinner parties every summer. Now Henry wants to do the same. Dinner in the garden among the flowers, under a full moon. Sounds fun.'

'What if it rains?' James said.

'It never rained for Henry's parents,' said Matthew.

'That was before the war.'

'The war has changed many things, but not the weather,' said Matthew. 'See you at Cotteshaw!'

————◇————

'I hear you're coming to Henry Tillotson's party,' Antonia said on the telephone to Barbara.

'Yes. Look, I'm in an awful hurry. I'm late for work.'

'Oh, work,' said Antonia. 'Actually, I hate my job.'

'Me too. All the hurrying in the morning, and coming home

10

exhausted every night to find the unwashed breakfast things, ugh!'

'Our parents think it's good for us. They're afraid we'll make mistakes if we marry too young.'

'I must go!' cried Barbara. 'See you at the weekend. Oh! Do you think we'll meet the mystery wife?'

'I hope so,' said Antonia. 'That's why I'm going.'

Minutes later, she was running down the street to the bus stop. It was true, her job was boring, and she missed the easy life in her parents' house. I shall marry soon, she thought, as the bus came. But who? Perhaps Matthew Stephenson would make a good husband. He's not very exciting, but he's kind. And Barbara? Antonia always made plans for her best friend as well as for herself. Barbara should marry James Martineau. He would make a good husband, too.

She laughed as she ran towards her boring office.

━━◈━━

Matthew was looking forward to the weekend. Driving down to Cotteshaw with Antonia beside him in the car, he thought how pretty she was. He had kissed her the evening before, and hoped to do so again.

'What's Henry's wife like?' she asked him.

'Beautiful, in a strange kind of way. I've only seen her once, for about five minutes. She doesn't often appear.'

'When did they marry?'

'During the war. They met in Egypt, I think. Her name is Margaret, by the way. Henry brought her to Cotteshaw, and she went to bed. And has stayed there ever since.'

'She isn't ill, but she lives in bed? She must be so bored!'

'Perhaps she is. If you meet her, you can ask her.'

'I will,' said Antonia. 'And if I don't, Barbara can.'

'No,' said Matthew quickly, 'don't. Don't ask her, or Henry. Just try to behave naturally and don't mention it.'

Just before they reached Cotteshaw, they saw James and Barbara, who had left their car and were standing by the gate to a field. Matthew stopped the car next to them.

'What are you two doing?' called Antonia.

'Just having a look at the view,' said James.

'Liar,' Barbara said. 'He stopped to ask me to marry him.'

'She refused me,' said James. 'But I shall try again. Come on. Let's all arrive at Cotteshaw together.'

James followed Matthew's car. 'What a nice house,' said Barbara as they stopped outside. While the two men got the luggage, the girls walked up to the open front door. They looked into a cool dark hall, full of the sweet smell of flowers.

'Hello,' a man's voice said. 'I'm Henry; you must be Antonia and Barbara. Don't let my dogs worry you,' he added, as the two dogs ran towards his guests.

Lovely girls, Henry thought, bright-eyed, not stupid. They know how pretty they are. He was pleased for his friends James and Matthew, but he could not stop himself wondering which of the girls would be most fun in bed.

The girls also studied Henry with interest. They saw long legs, black hair that needed cutting, and sharp black eyes.

'Rather nice,' whispered Antonia, as Henry went to say hello to Matthew and James.

12

'What a pity he's so old. He must be about thirty-five!'

'Well, I like older men.'

'So do I.'

Pilar took the girls to their rooms. As they went upstairs, something white flew past, and both girls screamed. A moment later they were laughing as a white cockatoo landed at the bottom of the stairs and walked calmly out of the door.

When they came downstairs, they went into the garden, where the young men were sitting at a table. Henry stood up. 'Come and have some tea,' he said. 'Pilar has made us some sandwiches. She tells me my wife's cockatoo frightened you.'

'Oh no, not at all,' said Antonia.

Conversation during tea was a little uncomfortable, she thought. It was difficult to forget that Henry's wife was lying in bed in one of the rooms upstairs. Was she listening to the sound of tea cups in the garden? Antonia wondered.

Then the cockatoo walked towards them across the grass, and said, 'Hello. Hello,' in its strange, high voice.

Everyone laughed. Matthew offered it a piece of cake, and Antonia asked, 'What's the bird's name? Did your wife give it a name?'

'I don't think she did,' said Henry. 'I gave it to her as a present, but I don't think she likes it. Why don't you ask her about it? Would you both like to meet her?'

'Of course we would,' said Barbara.

'Come on then. Let's do it now.'

He led them upstairs, knocked on a door, and opened it. 'Here are our visitors,' he said. 'Antonia and Barbara.'

'Come in,' said Margaret. 'How pleasant. Do sit down.'
Henry closed the door and they heard him walk away.

———◆◆◆———

The room was unlike anything the girls had ever seen. It was
an extraordinary room, a golden room full of silver mirrors.
The walls, carpet, curtains, bed-covers – everything was gold.
Even the woman in the bed, with her golden hair and silvery
eyes, seemed to be part of the colour plan.

'Do you like my room?' she asked. 'I've just had it done. I
get people from London to do it. They have to work around

'Hello. Hello,' said the cockatoo, in its strange, high voice.

14

me because I can't get out of bed. It was beautiful before, too, but I got tired of it. It was all black and white then. The mirrors were the same, of course. I like my mirrors.'

'What colour was it before that?' Antonia asked.

'Pink. It was all pink.'

'What does your husband think of the room?' said Barbara.

'I wouldn't know. I have not asked.'

'Will you wear a gold dress to the party?' asked Antonia.

Margaret narrowed her eyes. 'What party?'

'Oh dear,' said Antonia. 'I suppose Henry wanted it to be a surprise for you. How could we be so stupid?'

'I imagine that's quite easy for you both,' said Margaret.

Antonia gave a sudden shout of laughter.

'What have I said that's so funny?' said Margaret. 'Do you see that brush? You can brush my hair for me.'

'Brush it yourself,' Barbara said bravely. 'You have nothing else to do.'

In the garden, the men were surprised to hear laughter.

'Well,' Henry said, 'they seem to have found something to talk about. Look,' he went on, 'I have things to discuss with Trask. Will you two stay here and listen? Make sure nothing nasty happens?' He walked away, followed by the dogs.

'I hope the girls are all right,' James said. 'When I met Margaret, she told me that I was even more boring and stupid than her first husband. Then she asked me to open the window because she didn't like the way I smelled.'

'What do you think they're talking about?' said Matthew.

15

'Barbara will tell me,' said James. 'She tells me everything.'

'Are you going to marry her?' Matthew asked.

'I think so. I'm almost sure she'll accept me next time.'

James and Matthew sat on in the late afternoon sun, but the girls did not come down from Margaret's room until nearly an hour later. They seemed rather quiet, and avoided looking at Henry when he rejoined them.

Supper, a delicious meal cooked by Pilar, was eaten in the kitchen. Margaret, of course, had her meal in bed, Henry explained to his guests. He looked at Antonia and Barbara, smiling a little, and said, 'I must thank you girls for making my wife laugh. We heard your laughter from the garden.'

'We laughed. She didn't,' said Barbara. 'She hasn't much to laugh about,' she added quietly.

Everyone ate in silence for some moments, and although Pilar and Ebro soon began to talk about this and that, it was not a happy meal.

3
Engagements by moonlight

After supper, Matthew took Antonia out for a walk in the garden. He felt rather hurt and angry, and wanted to get away from the others.

'You and Barbara seem to be very friendly with Henry already,' he said. 'You stared at him all during supper, and when he spoke to you, you turned red.'

'That was the wine,' Antonia said. 'And I didn't stare.'

'You did. I was watching you.'

Antonia stopped and turned to look at him. Matthew took her face between his hands. Her skin was soft and fresh. 'Oh, Antonia.' He kissed her smooth young face. 'I apologize,' he said. 'You didn't stare. Will you marry me, Antonia?'

'Yes, I will. Gladly.' She put her arms round his neck.

In the tree above them the cockatoo gave a loud scream.

'That awful bird!' said Matthew. 'What a strange present for Henry to give his wife.'

'Have you seen her room?' said Antonia. 'I think your friend Henry keeps Margaret locked up there for his own horrible reasons. I'm so glad I'm marrying you.'

'We're going to be so happy together,' Matthew said.

'Not like that poor woman up there in her prison.'

'Oh God!' said Matthew. 'Do we have to talk about the Tillotsons? You can't seem to forget your visit to Margaret. What exactly did she say to you? You'd better tell me.'

'I will. Her first husband was a violent man, who beat her. When she divorced him, she met Henry. She didn't want to marry him, but he asked her again and again. He just wouldn't stop. Then, when she said yes, he brought her to live here, and put her in that room. She has no clothes, except nightdresses, and nothing to do. Her only amusement is having her room redecorated. It's so cruel. She didn't even know about the party he's giving.'

'My dear girl,' said Matthew. 'None of that is true.'

'Yes, it is. Barbara believes it too.'

'I think you girls should ask Henry what the truth is,' said Matthew.

'Perhaps I will.'

Matthew was tired of Henry's problems. 'Can we please talk about us?' he said. 'When shall we get married? Where shall we live? How many children shall we have?'

'Slow down!' cried Antonia, laughing. 'Let's start with a ring. Oh, Matthew! What fun it will all be!'

James had enjoyed his supper. Pilar was a good cook. As he ate, he watched Barbara and remembered the weekend a year ago, when he had brought Valerie to Cotteshaw. He had been so much in love with Valerie! Unfortunately, she had chosen to marry a man richer, more intelligent, and better-looking than himself. I will never allow myself to feel such pain again, he thought.

Later, as they walked in the garden together, Barbara said, 'When you asked me to marry you this afternoon, did you mean it? If you did, I'd like to say yes.'

'Of course I meant it,' James said.

They stopped walking, and James took her hands and kissed her. I shall be comfortable with Barbara, he thought. She will never hurt me as Valerie did.

'Do you love me?' Barbara asked.

'Of course.'

'Our marriage will not be like Henry's.'

'I hope not!'

Barbara said, 'Henry asked Margaret again and again to

18

marry him. He just wouldn't accept no for an answer. Would you stop asking me if I said no?'

'Of course not,' James lied.

They sat on a garden seat, holding hands, and a little later saw Henry coming back from walking his dogs.

'Oh, Henry!' Barbara called. 'We're engaged to be married. James would not accept no for an answer.'

'I hope you will be very happy,' said Henry. 'May I sit here with you, or would you rather be alone?'

'Sit with us. It's so lovely here in the moonlight,' said Barbara. 'Did you ask Margaret to marry you by moonlight?'

Henry said, 'No. It was in a bar. In Egypt.'

'Oh. How often did you have to ask her?'

'Just once,' Henry said. He stood up. 'Let's go in, it's too cold to sit out here.'

As they walked back to the house, they saw Antonia and Matthew, kissing under a tree. Antonia called out to them, 'Matthew and I are engaged. Isn't it wonderful?'

'Well, now, isn't that nice? Two happy couples,' said Henry. 'We must drink to this.' He went into the house to fetch a bottle and glasses. As he put them on the garden table, the cockatoo flew down and sat on his arm.

'Where did you get that bird?' asked Antonia.

'From a shop. I hate seeing wild things in prison like that. Birds should be free. All living things need to be free.'

The girls looked at one another disbelievingly. Henry saw the look, and laughed. 'You think my wife is my prisoner,' he said, 'but she is free to do anything she wants. Now, let's drink

19

'Well, now, isn't that nice? Two happy couples.'

to your future. I hope you all come again often, and when you have children, that you will bring them too. This is a good place for children.'

Before they went to sleep, the two girls sat on Antonia's bed and talked. 'Antonia Stephenson,' said Antonia. 'How does it sound? And Barbara Martineau. They're both good names.'

'Tillotson,' said Barbara.

'What?'

'I can't stop thinking about Margaret,' said Barbara.

Antonia said, 'It isn't Margaret I've been thinking about. It's Henry. Did you talk to James about him?'

'No. We were too busy talking about getting married.'

'Did you tell James what Margaret said about Henry and the awful things he does? You know, with men. And horses.'

'No. I couldn't say that to James. Did *you* tell Matthew?'

'Of course not,' said Antonia. 'So all the time you and James were talking about getting married, you were thinking about Henry Tillotson.'

'Not all the time, but yes, a bit. And you were, too.'

'Yes,' said Antonia. 'It's hard *not* to think about him.'

'But you do love Matthew,' said Barbara.

'Of course,' Antonia said. 'Do you love James?'

'Yes. Of course I do.'

'So why are we discussing Henry?'

—◆◇◆—

When the girls woke up next morning, they could hear people in the garden, getting things ready for the party. Trask and Ebro were bringing out tables and pushing them together to make one long one. Then Henry came out, and began to talk to Pilar about flowers. The girls looked down from their open window, watching it all, and chatting to each other.

21

Suddenly, Henry looked up. 'Are you two girls going to stay there all morning, or would you like to come for a drive before breakfast? I could take you out in my Bentley.'

'Ooh!' said Barbara. 'Is it one of those lovely old Bentleys?'

'1926. It was my father's.'

'Wow!' Antonia said. 'We'll be down in two minutes.'

As they drove along the narrow country roads past the fields of Henry's farm, he asked, 'What will your parents say about your engagements? Will they be pleased?'

'Oh, yes,' said Antonia. 'They've been afraid that we'd fall in love with someone with no money.'

'They don't really know us,' Barbara said. 'We decided a long time ago to find husbands who can take good care of us.'

'I see. Do James and Matthew know this?'

'I think they'd agree with us,' said Barbara. 'We don't need life to be perfect. We prefer to be comfortable.'

'I expect you're right,' said Henry. 'Look, over there is the lake. I often ride there from the house and have a swim.'

'Does your wife ever go with you?' said Barbara.

'My wife doesn't like horses. Listen,' he went on. 'Could you two do something for me? Well, two things, actually.'

'Of course. What?' the girls said.

'Pick some flowers for the dinner table.' After a pause he added, 'And, well, I've bought a dress for my wife. Could one of you pretend it's yours, and offer to lend it to her for the party?'

'But she never gets out of bed!' said Barbara.

'There are times . . . I had hoped . . .'

22

'Of course we'll try,' said Antonia. 'And we'll do the flowers.'

'Don't you think we are sensible to choose safe husbands? Not to marry *just* for love?' Barbara asked. 'We shall probably have happy marriages.'

'What hard little heads on young shoulders,' Henry said.

'We are almost twenty, Henry.'

He laughed. 'I wonder what your children will be like.'

———◇◇◇———

James and Matthew, later in the morning, were in Matthew's car, going to collect ice and strawberries for the party.

'Henry's farm is looking good,' James said. 'I'd like to live in the country, but London is where the jobs are.'

Matthew said, 'The country is all right for holidays.'

'And weekends. I shall bring Barbara here again. We may come often.'

'I thought you liked to go sailing at weekends.'

'I do, but Barbara doesn't. I could send her here while I go off on my boat. And of course we will start a family soon.'

'Oh. Is that what Barbara wants?'

'I haven't discussed it with her yet,' said James. 'But I think, don't you, it's best to do all that while we're young. Then we can have fun later, go travelling, that sort of thing.'

'Was that how you'd planned your life with Valerie?'

'Oh, Valerie. Valerie was different,' James said.

Life with Valerie was too painful to think about. With Barbara it will be different, James thought. She's young and inexperienced, and I will be the boss.

23

I shouldn't be cruel to him, Matthew thought. He's still in love with Valerie. 'You and Barbara make a great couple,' he said kindly. 'She's a lovely girl.'

'So is Antonia,' said James. 'I think you're very lucky.'

'Yes. My parents will be pleased. My father has been advising me to get married. I really need a wife, to do business dinner parties for me, and so on. And, of course, I'm very much in love with Antonia.'

'Yes, we're both lucky,' James said. 'Unlike poor Henry.'

'I expect his father never gave him any sensible advice,' said Matthew.

4
The dinner party

'Who else is coming to the party, Henry?' James asked, as the three men carried the ice into the kitchen.

'Hector and Calypso. They've just got back from Italy. The two Jonathans – you've met them before. And Peter and Maisie Bullivant, old friends from the village.'

'They say Calypso was very beautiful when she was a girl,' James said. 'Broke a lot of hearts, I heard. Did you know her then, Henry? You're about the same age.'

'I'm a few years younger. Yes, she's an old friend.'

How I loved her, Henry thought. I loved the very ground she walked on, but she never knew. She married Hector early in the war, married him for his money, so she said – a man old enough to be her father. When I heard that news in a bar in Cairo, thought Henry, I went out and got very, very drunk. And the next day, I got father's letter.

— ◇◇◇ —

In the kitchen Pilar was working hard. She wanted it to be a perfect party, as good as the parties Henry's parents had given. Every time she looked at Henry, she remembered his father, who had found her and her sick baby in a refugee camp in France, and had saved their lives. Her husband was dead, and she had wanted to die, too. Henry's father had changed all that, and she would never forget his kindness.

Henry had been away at the war when his father died. Pilar had been the old man's nurse during his final days. 'What shall I do without you?' she had asked him.

'Stay here and take care of Henry.'

'What if he brings home a wife?'

'Ah yes. I wrote to him. He may get married. Do you see that letter on the table? Please post it, Pilar. And tell him about my death.'

When he died, she had kissed him and closed his eyes. Then she had gone out to post the letter. Why did I do it? she thought. Why didn't I just throw it away?

Upstairs, she heard Margaret's bell, and went to see what she wanted. Margaret was standing by the window, watching Antonia and Barbara as they played with Henry's dogs.

'Which girl is James Martineau's?' she asked.

'The one with brown hair.'

'She's not as pretty as Valerie. Is he in love with her?'

'I do not know.'

'Of course you don't,' said Margaret. 'What could you know about love?'

Pilar said, 'I leave you now. I am busy.' These women, she thought, they know nothing. She thought of the love she had felt for her young husband and how desperately she still missed him.

She had read the letter Henry's father had written. Then she had posted it, because he had asked her to. Now she could not forgive herself for posting it.

—◦◦◦◦—

The girls had arranged the flowers they had picked and were now putting them on the table in the garden. Henry came out to look.

'Wonderful, all roses! Very pretty,' he said, thinking, my God, they've picked every single rose in the garden. 'Now, come and see the dress I bought for Margaret. It's from Dior.'

'Dior!' and 'Wow!' cried the girls together.

They ran into the house, and as Henry followed them, the cockatoo flew past him. He tried to catch it, but it escaped through a window. 'I must catch him before the party,' he said. 'He sometimes tries to bite people.'

'Catch him later! We want to see the dress!'

Henry led them to his room, which was large and sunny, with bookshelves and comfortable old armchairs and a big bed. I like the bed, Antonia thought. Henry can lie there and look out over his fields. I'd like to sleep here. Then she thought, I must stop this. I am in love with Matthew.

'What a lovely room,' Barbara said. 'You can lie here and watch your horses in the field. Are you very fond of your horses, Henry?' As she spoke, she turned a little red, remembering what Margaret had said.

Henry looked at her. 'I see my wife has been saying nasty things about me,' he said coolly.

For a moment neither girl knew what to say, and they avoided meeting Henry's eyes. At last Barbara whispered, almost tearfully, 'The dress?'

Henry brought it out and the girls stared at it. It was beautiful, light and soft, the colour of a flame. 'Pretend it's yours,' Henry said, watching their faces. 'Persuade her to get out of bed and wear it tonight.'

'It's lovely. If she doesn't, she must be mad,' Antonia said.

Barbara held the dress against her body. 'There's no mirror in this room,' she said. 'How does it look?'

Antonia did not like the way her friend was looking at Henry. 'There are lots of mirrors in Margaret's room. Let's take it to her. I expect Henry's busy, aren't you, Henry?'

Henry thought how good the dress would look with either Barbara's brown hair or Antonia's fair skin. 'Well, good luck,' he said, and went downstairs, followed by his dogs.

'What she said about the horses can't be true,' Antonia whispered. 'I think it's the dogs!' They both started laughing, and found they could not stop.

They did not laugh, however, in Margaret's room. She had listened stony-faced to their little story about the dress, and now they sat side by side on the golden sofa, watching her as she sat in her golden bed. Across a chair the Dior dress lay like an exhausted ghost.

'Aren't you going to put the dress on?' Barbara asked.

'Why should I want to?' said Margaret. Then Antonia and Barbara heard her say something very quietly, which sounded rather like, 'What a nasty pair of girls.'

Antonia picked the dress up and held it against herself. 'So many mirrors,' she said. 'All in your room.'

'The Jonathans found them for me.' Margaret watched her.

'Who are the Jonathans?' asked Barbara.

'Two old queers, just like him,' said Margaret.

It was strange, Barbara thought, how she never used Henry's name. It was always 'he' or 'him'.

'That dress would look good on Valerie,' Margaret said, watching Barbara. 'James Martineau's girl. He was very much in love with her. When they visited, they had a room near mine, made a lot of noise at night.' She laughed. 'Leave the dress with me,' she said to Antonia.

Antonia, seeing her friend's shocked face, said, 'You know, Margaret, you should wear this dress. It's a nice colour for an older woman. Very kind to older skin.'

She opened a cupboard door to put the dress away. 'Oh, look!' she said. 'You have hundreds of clothes! What a liar you are!'

'Close the curtains before you go,' Margaret said. 'The sun is in my eyes.'

'Close them yourself. We'll see you at the party tonight.'

'I shan't be there.'

Antonia picked the dress up and held it against herself.

Outside the door, Barbara said, 'Who is Valerie?'

'Nobody. It's all lies. Nothing she says is true.'

'Oh. Do you really think so?'

Waiting for his guests to arrive, Henry wondered why he was giving this party. Was it because his parents had given them in the past? He looked at the dinner table with its glass and silver, the tall candles and the flowers, and remembered his mother. She had died too young. And without her, there had been nobody to stop his father's wild ideas.

If his mother were alive now, what would she say? Would she suggest a divorce, or would she recognize that it was impossible? Margaret did nothing which in law could be a cause for him to divorce her, and she had already refused to divorce him. He had talked to a lawyer once, and he knew that there was no easy way to end this sad marriage.

'Henry, you look wonderful.' Calypso appeared, and put her hand through his arm. 'What are you doing?'

'Thinking about murdering my wife.' He was glad Calypso had never known how much he loved her. These days they were good friends.

She laughed. 'How can we help?'

Hector came out and joined them. 'Good to see you,' he said, shaking Henry's hand. 'Is Margaret coming to the party? Any pretty girls?'

Henry said, 'Matthew Stephenson has brought Antonia Lowther, and Barbara O'Malley is with James Martineau. Both couples got themselves engaged last night. As for

Margaret, there is a place for her at the table, and she has a new dress. Now she must decide.'

He began to open wine bottles. 'The girls, Antonia and Barbara, have met Margaret,' he said. 'And she's changed her room again. It's all gold now.'

'And does she still lie in bed all day,' asked Hector, 'expecting everyone to be her servant?'

'Hector, stop it!' said Calypso. 'I blame your father,' she said to Henry.

'He had nothing to do with it,' said Henry.

'Yes, he did. He made you too kind to other people, too nice to everyone.'

Pilar was now bringing the food out to the long table, and suddenly the two girls, one in a pink dress and the other in blue, ran out of the house, followed by the two young men. As Henry began introductions, Peter and Maisie Bullivant and the Jonathans arrived in a noisy group.

'Calypso, my dear!' the Jonathans cried. 'Beautiful as ever! May we kiss you? Oh, look at those wonderful fish on the table. They look so pretty, it will be a crime to eat them!'

When everyone had a drink in their hand, Barbara found herself talking to the Jonathans. 'James and I have just got engaged,' she told them. 'And so has Antonia, to Matthew.'

'How nice. You must let us advise you all on beds,' said Jonathan. 'So important to buy a good bed when you're married. I see that your future husband is a big man and you are quite small. It's the same with me and John. If you don't have a good bed, and one of you is much heavier—'

'Time to eat, I think,' said James, not pleased at this rather personal advice to his future wife.

Henry went around the table with the wine, and Pilar and Ebro brought out the soup. Both were dressed in black, Ebro with a red tie, and Pilar with a red flower in her hair. 'My dears, how lovely!' the Jonathans cried.

Everyone sat down at the table, finding their own places. Antonia and Barbara ran to sit next to Henry, leaving James and Matthew to sit on the other side of the table. Trask, Pilar, and Ebro sat down to eat, too.

Soon all the guests were chatting happily. Calypso was amused to see how the two girls seemed more interested in Henry than in the young men they were engaged to. No one mentioned the absent Margaret until Peter Bullivant, not a sensitive man, called out to Henry at the head of the table.

'I hear,' he said, 'that your wife has changed her room again, to gold this time. Must cost you a fortune.'

'It's not polite to talk about money, Peter,' Maisie said.

'What? Don't try to tell me what I can talk about!'

'Well, it's true.'

'I love the way you two quarrel in front of everyone,' said Jonathan. 'Rather sweet, really.'

'What was I saying before my stupid wife stopped me?' Peter asked. 'Well, anyway. Wonderful party, Henry. Excellent food and wine.'

'He could tell you exactly how much it all cost,' Maisie said proudly. 'He's awfully clever. And it's all right if you do it in private.'

Everyone laughed, and then conversation became general while people ate the wonderful fish that Pilar had cooked so beautifully. From time to time Henry circled the table, moving in and out of the shadows, refilling his guests' glasses, and listening to bits of conversation as he passed.

5
A late arrival

Calypso was the first to see Margaret. It was now quite dark, and the candlelight threw mysterious shadows around the table. But one of the shadows, Calypso thought, was Margaret, watching and listening in the dark.

'Hector,' she said, in a low voice, 'look who's here.'

Hector looked. 'I see her. I wonder what she's planning,' he whispered, and closed his fingers over his wife's hand.

Peter and Maisie were arguing noisily with the Jonathans. Henry got up to refill glasses, and asked the girls to collect the fish plates, which left three empty chairs. It was at that moment that the cockatoo jumped down onto the table with a loud scream.

Everyone jumped, then laughed, but when the excitement was over, it was a much greater shock to see Margaret seated at the head of the table. She smiled at them all.

'So sorry to be late,' she said. 'Is there any fish for me?'

They all stared at her. She was wearing the Dior dress, and her golden hair, freshly brushed, looked beautiful.

33

'You had your fish in your room, hours ago,' Trask said.

'Dear Trask, I did, but now I'd like some more.'

'None left,' said Henry. 'Have some strawberries. Jonathan and John, why don't you go and sit next to Margaret?'

They did so, and filled her plate with strawberries and her

Margaret smiled at the Jonathans. 'Dear boys,' she said.

glass with wine. Margaret smiled at them. 'Dear boys,' she said. 'Dear Jonathan, and dear John.'

For a while everything seemed pleasant, and then, in answer to a question from James, Margaret began to talk about herself. The others listened wide-eyed.

'I was married to a man who beat me, who stole my money, and who drank,' she began.

Henry laughed and stood up. 'Come for a walk,' he said to Calypso and Hector. 'I've heard the story before.'

'Don't laugh,' said Calypso. 'It isn't funny. And I don't expect any of it is true.'

As they walked away from the table, Barbara jumped up and followed them. Henry turned to see her behind them.

'You were not invited,' he said, 'but as you've chosen to join us, you can listen. You've heard my wife's lies. Now I'll tell you the truth.'

'How did it start?' Calypso asked.

'Love,' Henry said. 'For years and years I was in love with a girl. She was older than me, very lovely, always surrounded by other men, and had no idea how I felt.'

'And what happened?' Hector asked.

'The war happened. I was in Cairo, and one day I received two letters. One was from the Jonathans, who told me that the girl I loved was married. The other letter was from my father. He told me he was dying, and asked for my help. There was an Englishwoman in Cairo, who had been married to a German, but was now divorced. There was a danger that the British would put her in prison, and he very much wanted to help her. As he was dying, he could do nothing himself, so he asked me to save her by marrying her.'

'And it was Margaret,' said Hector.

Calypso said, 'But it was so *stupid* of you to agree to it!'

'I suppose you thought, why not?' said Hector. 'You'd lost your girl, and you expected to get killed anyway.'

'That kind of thing,' said Henry. 'And now I'd better get back to my party. And you, Barbara, had better get back to James. Come on. Calypso and Hector can follow us.'

As they walked, Barbara said, 'Henry, tell me about Valerie. Was James in love with her?'

'Valerie? How do you know about her?'

'Your wife told me.'

'That woman causes so much trouble!' said Henry. 'Forget Valerie. She meant nothing to James. He's in love with you. You love him, don't you?'

'Yes,' said Barbara uncertainly. 'But I wanted to ask . . .'

Barbara's question was never asked, because just then they heard screams and shouts coming from the dinner party. Henry began to run.

—◈—

The dinner table looked like a battlefield. Candles and glasses had been knocked over, flowers lay everywhere, and Margaret danced along the table, holding in one hand the broken and bloody body of the white cockatoo.

Maisie and Pilar were screaming, and Peter was being sick behind a chair. The other men tried to catch Margaret, but she avoided them easily. Then Antonia jumped up on the table. Margaret laughed at her. 'Come on!' she cried, and, pulling off the bird's head, threw it into Antonia's face.

At that moment, Henry threw himself on the table, catching Margaret round the knees. The table fell over, and they crashed to the ground in a shower of broken glass and plates. As she fell, Margaret bit Henry on the neck.

The screaming stopped, and there was silence in the garden. Then Henry said, 'Are you hurt, Margaret? You must not get cold.' He put his jacket around her and led her to the house. As they went, she said, 'Good night, everyone. That was a good party. I did enjoy it.'

Gently, Henry helped Margaret into her bed. She looked around her at the golden room and said, 'I'm tired of this colour. I shall change it again, the Jonathans will help me. You are as useless as those two old queers. Why did you marry me? You have no idea how to behave to a woman. You prefer your animals to me.'

Henry said, 'Margaret, you know I married you because you needed a British passport. My father asked me to help you, to save you from prison.'

'Stupid old man.'

'He was not stupid. He was kind.'

'Rubbish. The old queers, the Jonathans, made him ask you to help me.'

What was the truth? Henry wondered.

'You cannot divorce me,' Margaret said. 'You will never be free of me, and you will never have children. I shall make certain of that.'

The screaming stopped, and there was silence in the garden.

He put up a hand and touched the blood on his neck. 'Try and sleep now,' he said. 'Good night.'

'I am glad I bit you,' his wife said.

Nobody spoke very much as they collected broken glass and tidied the garden. Maisie and Peter whispered their goodbyes and went home. The Jonathans followed soon after.

Then Antonia lifted a plate, and there was the cockatoo's head. 'Oh God!' she cried. 'She threw it in my face!'

'It's all right,' said Matthew. 'It's over now. Let me . . .'

'You enjoyed it,' Antonia said accusingly. 'You liked it when she started dancing on the table. You found it amusing. How could you?' she screamed. 'God! Why did I ever get engaged to you?'

'Bedtime, girls,' Hector said. 'Off you go.'

Barbara took Antonia by the hand and led her away. Matthew and James followed them.

Halfway to the house Antonia turned and shouted, 'How can Henry be so forgiving?'

'How indeed?' said Calypso quietly.

Henry came down from Margaret's bedroom looking surprisingly calm. 'Tonight was my fault,' he said to Hector and Calypso. 'I must let her stay in bed and get up only when she chooses to.'

'Can't you divorce her?' said Hector.

'For killing a cockatoo? And who would take care of her if I did? No,' Henry said, 'I can't divorce her.'

As they walked to the house, James took Barbara's hand, and pulled her away from Antonia. 'You disappeared,' he said. 'Where did you go?'

'I was with Henry.'

'Oh! Why? Why are you chasing him?'

Barbara replied angrily, with a question about Valerie, and they were soon locked in a violent quarrel. There were accusations and tears, and a few lies were told, but in the end they kissed and went off to their own rooms.

Antonia and Matthew also quarrelled that night. Matthew made Antonia so angry that she wanted to hit him, and yet, she thought, I suppose I shall marry him. She was desperate for a hot bath, and when she found Barbara in their shared bathroom, she banged on the door. But Barbara refused to let her in, and Antonia, after shouting angrily at her friend through the keyhole, ran off to search the house for an empty bathroom.

The next morning James and Matthew met in the kitchen. Henry was out, working on the farm, and Pilar was cooking breakfast. Matthew felt ill, after too much wine the night before, and could only drink black coffee, but James was enjoying a delicious plate of eggs. 'You should drink plenty of water after a party,' he told Matthew. 'I always do.' It was something Valerie had taught him. Matthew looked at him with dislike and drank his black coffee carefully.

'What a beautiful day. That coffee smells wonderful,' Antonia said, as she and Barbara came into the kitchen. She went and put her arm around Matthew. 'I was horrible to you last night. I'm very sorry.'

'You were tired,' said Matthew. 'And you'd been so brave.'

'Enough about last night,' said Pilar. 'Today is a new day.'

I am learning, Antonia thought. I shall be a clever wife.

'We must visit Margaret,' said Barbara, cutting some bread. 'Poor woman. She must be feeling awful this morning.'

There was a surprised silence. Well! thought James. I can't imagine Valerie ever saying something like that.

'And James,' Barbara went on, 'you haven't said good morning yet. I think it's important to be polite, don't you?'

Pilar watched them, amused. 'You make a good start. You will all have happy marriages, like Hector and Calypso.'

'Oh Pilar!' the girls cried. 'Calypso married Hector for his money. Everybody knows that. She wasn't in love, as we are.'

'It's a good marriage,' Pilar said. 'Try to be as happy as they are when you marry.'

—◆—

James and Barbara found Margaret sitting up in bed, looking young and beautiful.

'Wasn't it a lovely party?' she said. 'Henry was so kind to surprise me like that. He's so good to me.'

Barbara opened her mouth to speak, but Margaret went on, 'I have been thinking. It's good for Henry to have you all here. The poor man is lonely with me in bed all day and only the servants to talk to. And he's so generous. He gives these wonderful parties, although the house is shabby and he has

41

no money. Wouldn't it be sensible if all the friends who come here at weekends with their girls paid him something? What do you think of that?'

'That was a surprise,' Barbara said as she and James went downstairs.

'And it's a good idea, too,' said James. 'We could all come here at weekends, as paying guests. It would help Henry.'

'James, she's crazy. She doesn't mean what she says. And I don't think sharing Henry's house is a good idea.'

'Why not? It's an excellent idea,' he said. 'We'll bring our children here. And if you don't like sailing, you could come here while I sail.'

They walked towards the lake. It was a warm, sunny morning, and they found Antonia and Matthew already sitting there. Matthew liked Margaret's idea, too. 'We'll discuss it with Henry,' he said. 'I must say, I'd enjoy having a private lake! Coming for a swim, James?'

The two girls watched as the young men swam across the lake. 'We may come back to Cotteshaw, then,' Antonia said. She began to laugh. 'Where will this lead us, Barbara?'

PART THREE

6

Barbara's problem and Antonia's boredom

Four years later, there had been changes at Cotteshaw. Antonia and Matthew came often for weekends, bringing their baby daughter, Susie. James and Barbara, who had no children yet, came less often. Pilar loved babies, and was always happy to help Antonia with Susie. It made a change for her from taking care of Margaret, who remained in bed.

The Jonathans now rented part of Henry's garden. They grew vegetables there, and sold them in the local market, together with their eggs and chickens. The weekend visitors also paid rent for the rooms they used, which meant there was more money coming in. Cotteshaw was less shabby and more comfortable than it had been for many years.

Henry's life was quiet. He worked on his farm, and occasionally went to London. When he did, he always brought back an expensive present for Margaret, which she usually threw at somebody.

He was in London one weekend while Antonia, Matthew, and Susie were at Cotteshaw. He visited his bank, did some shopping, and took a box of potatoes to James and Barbara's house. When he rang the bell, Barbara came to the door.

'I've brought the potatoes you wanted from the Jonathans,' he said, noticing that her eyes were red from crying.

'Oh, thanks,' Barbara said, and began to close the door.

Henry put his foot in the door. 'What's the matter, Barbara? What's wrong?'

'Nothing.'

'Where's James?'

Tears began to run down Barbara's face.

'Sailing.'

'Who with?'

Tears began to run down her face. Henry stepped inside, put his arms around her, and held her close. Barbara put her head on his shoulder and cried, making his shirt wet.

Later, when Barbara could speak again, Henry asked, 'What have you and James been quarrelling about?'

'It's because James wants a baby,' said Barbara, 'and we can't have one. He says it's my fault, but, you see, I know he went to a doctor. I read his private letters about tests he'd had, and I know it's *his* fault. He only has a one in ten chance of fathering a child. When he found out that I'd read his letters, he just exploded. Then he rang Valerie, and now he's gone sailing with her.'

'Mm,' said Henry. 'Come on, I'll take you out to lunch.'

'I can't come out with my face like this.'

'Yes, you can, don't argue. Put some dark glasses on.'

Over a delicious lunch with cool white wine, Henry told her about Valerie. 'She's really rather boring,' he said, 'and she's starting to get fat. James knew her a long time ago, before he met you.'

'I love James,' Barbara said. 'I wasn't in love with him when I married him, but I am now. I want to make him happy, but I just disappoint him.'

They came out of the restaurant into bright sunshine. Henry took Barbara's arm and they walked home.

'Time for a little sleep,' said Henry. He led Barbara upstairs to the bedroom and helped her undress.

Afterwards Barbara said, 'Mm, that was lovely. I'm sorry I laughed.'

'Why shouldn't you laugh? Half the fun of bed is laughter,' said Henry. He turned on his side. 'Go to sleep now.'

When Barbara woke up, Henry was gone. As she got out of bed, the phone rang. It was Antonia.

'Aren't you coming down to Cotteshaw this weekend? Do come. I'm bored here without you.'

'I've got a bad headache. Perhaps I'll come tomorrow,' Barbara said. 'I'll see.'

She felt calm and happy. She was lying in a warm bath when she heard the front door open, and James ran upstairs. He came into the bathroom, his face white.

'Thank God you're here,' he said. 'I feel so ashamed. Oh, Barbara, I've had an awful day. I pretended I was going to see Valerie, but it wasn't true. I've been alone on my boat, thinking about you all day. I love you so much.'

'It's all right, my love,' Barbara said. 'I love you too. We love one another. Nothing else matters.'

Valerie was forgotten. James knew that he had fallen in love with Barbara, and that he would never love anyone else.

————◇◇◇————

Antonia was lonely at Cotteshaw without Barbara. Henry was in London, Matthew had gone for a walk, and Pilar was playing with Susie. Antonia decided to visit Margaret. She hated doing it on her own, but felt she had to do it.

Margaret had not changed in four years. She said nasty things about Susie, and laughed unpleasantly when Antonia asked if she ever got bored staying in her room all the time.

'Bored?' she said. '*You* should know about boredom. You must be bored with your husband by now. I'm sure he's bored with you.'

How does she know how I feel about Matthew? Antonia wondered, as she cooked the supper.

When Henry returned from London, looking cheerful, and bringing a bottle of expensive perfume for Margaret, Antonia told him, 'I phoned Barbara. She hasn't come down because she has a bad headache. But she never usually gets headaches, and I think it's because she's pregnant at last.'

Henry seemed amused, but wouldn't tell Antonia what he was smiling about. Antonia felt cross, and had the feeling he was laughing at her.

When Matthew came in from his walk, they sat down to have dinner. Suddenly, Antonia was annoyed by everything Matthew said and did. Why did he put so much food into his mouth? How could he open bottles of Henry's wine without asking Henry first? He was so stupid and rude! Even his clothes were boring, she thought, looking at Henry's old but much more interesting clothes.

The meal was nearly finished when Matthew said, 'I've been thinking, Henry. We shall soon need to use another room in this house. Antonia and I are planning to have a son.'

'*You've* been thinking?' she said angrily. 'Matthew—'

'Please, my dear,' said Matthew, 'Let me speak to Henry.' He drank some wine and went on, 'I shall pay you for the extra room, of course.'

They were all looking at Matthew, and it was at that moment that Margaret walked into the room. She went straight to the side table, picked up the bottle of perfume, opened it, and threw the perfume all over the dogs.

—◈—

'No!' cried the Jonathans. 'Poor old dogs! Go on, Antonia, what happened next? Tell us everything!'

'Well,' said Antonia, drinking black coffee, 'Henry laughed and offered her a glass of wine. We'd all had quite a lot of wine already. And then Matthew put his arm round Margaret, all sweet and kind, and said, "What's the trouble, my dear?" And then – listen to this, boys – she kissed him and he kissed her back.'

'So you were cross with Matthew,' the Jonathans said.

'Cross!' cried Antonia. 'I wanted to murder him! Anyway, I had to talk to somebody, so I ran out and phoned Barbara. But she was no help. She couldn't talk, she said, because she and James were leaving for Paris in about five minutes. Don't *laugh*, boys, it's not *funny*.'

'We're not laughing,' they said, laughing helplessly. 'It's a very sad story. Terrible. What happened next, Antonia?'

'Henry had disappeared, with his dogs,' Antonia went on. 'And then I saw Matthew helping Margaret up the stairs to her room. I was desperate. I went upstairs, I collected Susie, put a blanket round her, put her in the car, and drove off into the night. I ended up at Hector and Calypso's house, and I spent the rest of the night there. And now I've come here.'

'Well,' said the older Jonathan. 'Your husband's already

48

been here, looking for you. He looked quite ill with worry, poor man. And he said he loved you, if that helps.'

'Huh!' said Antonia.

'You'll probably find him at the Bullivants' house,' said the younger man. 'He went to see if you were there. Shall we give them a ring?'

———◈———

Henry woke up in the field by his lake. It was still dark, and he felt cold. Beside him, his dogs slept.

As the birds began to sing, he stood up and started to walk home. He had come out the night before, he remembered, desperate to escape from his wife, his paying guests, his whole life. In the warm summer air, he had fallen asleep.

The sky grew red. It was going to be a hot day. As he passed the wood, he remembered how, as a boy, he had hidden in that wood and dreamed of Calypso. She had broken his heart then; now she and Hector were his dear friends. What a strong, clever, sensible woman she was. More sensible than those two girls, he thought. They were not making a success of their marriages. 'And I,' he said out loud to his dogs, 'am not helping them either.'

He felt happy and peaceful this morning, and he had stopped being angry with Margaret. Life could be worse. In some strange way, she gave him freedom.

Soon he saw Trask, coming out to work in the fields. Trask liked to be the bringer of bad news.

'So there you are,' he shouted to Henry. 'You'll want to get back home. That Antonia has taken the baby and driven away

49

with her. Matthew took Margaret upstairs, fell asleep on her bed and spent the night in her room, Pilar says. Now he's taken your Bentley to go and look for his wife and baby.'

Henry laughed.

Three or four weeks later Antonia was sitting on a crowded bus in London. It was a rainy day, with a strong wind that was blowing umbrellas inside out. Suddenly she saw Henry walking along the street. 'I must get off!' she shouted, and before the bus had stopped, she threw herself off it and landed in the road at Henry's feet.

'Whatever did you do that for?' said Henry, helping her to her feet. 'Have you hurt yourself?'

'Banged my knees. Saw you from the bus,' said Antonia, a little shaken.

'You've got dirt all down your coat and your legs,' said Henry. 'Look, I'm staying at a friend's flat just round the corner. She's out at the moment, but you can clean yourself up there. And then how about some lunch?'

Antonia said, 'Lunch would be lovely.'

While Antonia washed, Henry asked her through the bathroom door, 'What was the crazy idea that made you jump off that bus?'

'I've just been to visit my mother,' Antonia said. 'She's been telling me how to manage my life. Be sensible. Think carefully before you do anything. When I saw you from the bus, I decided in half a second that I would do something I've wanted to do for a long time – ask you to make love to me.'

'And then how about some lunch?' said Henry.

There was a short pause. Then Henry said, 'Why not now, before lunch?'

'In your friend's bed?' said Antonia.

'If you prefer, we can use the floor,' said Henry. 'Personally, I'd rather be comfortable.'

◆◇◆

Almost ten years later Antonia talked to Calypso about that day. 'Henry saved my marriage,' she said.

She had come over from Cotteshaw to visit, bringing her two daughters, Susie and Clio, now aged twelve and nine, and Hilaria, who was Barbara's daughter. The little girls were playing in the wood that Hector had planted.

'I've never told anyone about this before,' said Antonia, knowing that secrets told to Calypso were never passed on. 'I love Matthew, of course I do, but I was so bored with him at that time. All he could talk about was the son he wanted. I was miserable, and taking life much too seriously. Meeting Henry that day did me so much good – he was kind, he was amusing, and we had *fun*. And after we'd made love, I decided I would never leave Matthew and I would make a success of my marriage. That's what Henry helped me to do.'

'Did you never talk to your friend Barbara about this?'

'No,' Antonia said. 'That was the time when she and James suddenly fell in love all over again and went off to Paris. After that Barbara was pregnant with Hilaria, and she had less time for me. I just couldn't tell her that I'd slept with Henry, nor that we did it again from time to time. Poor Henry, what a disappointing life he's had with that awful woman . . .'

Calypso was tired of listening to this. 'I don't think Henry is a disappointed person. He's been a good friend to you, and very kind to your children. They are lovely children,' she added more kindly. 'Henry seems very fond of them.'

'Oh yes,' said Antonia, 'he's wonderful with them. And we all think it's good for him, with no children of his own, to have a share in ours.'

7

Two daughters are born

One winter afternoon at Cotteshaw, after a visit to Margaret, the Jonathans came downstairs laughing, and went into the kitchen to talk to Pilar.

'Oh, Pilar,' they said. 'It's awful! Terrible!'

Margaret's room was now red – red walls, red ceiling, red furniture, red curtains, and the mirrors made it even worse.

'And it's all our fault,' said the Jonathans. 'We persuaded her to get out of bed and then took her shopping in London.'

'And the red dress, did you see the red dress?' Pilar asked. 'Margaret likes to walk around now, to show us her beautiful small waist.' She laughed, and pointed out of the window, where they could see Barbara and Antonia walking together.

The two girls no longer had waists. They were both heavily pregnant and could only wear shapeless clothes.

'They do look quite funny,' said Jonathan. 'I expect Margaret enjoys laughing at them.'

On their way home they saw James, also out walking. 'He looks so pleased with himself, have you noticed?' said John. 'You'd think nobody had ever been a father before.'

James was, indeed, deeply happy. To him, Barbara was more beautiful than she had ever been, and he was full of love for her and for his unborn child. The Jonathans could never understand that, he thought, waving at them as he passed.

At the back door he met Henry, coming in from the fields. He told Henry how happy he was, and Henry, a kind man, said, 'I am glad.' But even he, thought James, will never really know how I feel. He felt sorry for his poor, childless friend.

———◆———

Two weeks before Barbara's baby was expected, she and James were at Cotteshaw. She wanted, she told Antonia, to know what to expect.

'You've been through it already,' she said. 'And James is so nervous that it will be good for him to talk to Matthew.'

'I don't know about that,' said Antonia. 'Henry is more help. He gives them both jobs to do on the farm, to stop them telling us what to do all the time.'

'Henry is a thoughtful and generous man,' Barbara said, 'and I'm grateful.'

'I suppose he is.' Antonia smiled. 'Yes, you're right.'

'Tell me about the pain,' Barbara said. 'I'm not very good with pain, never have been.'

'You forget all about it when it's over,' Antonia said. 'You're just so happy to have the baby.'

'And I suppose Matthew was delighted,' Barbara said.

'To be honest, Matthew wanted a son.'

'I'm sure you'll have a boy this time,' said Barbara. 'I'm lucky. James will be delighted with a boy or a girl.'

'If it's not a boy,' Antonia said, 'Matthew will just have to accept it. Two children is enough. I'm not having any more.'

They were walking slowly round the lake. It was a cold

winter day, and a little powdery snow lay on the grass. Susie, who was now three years old, played in the snow, running and jumping around the women's feet. 'Keep away from the water,' her mother warned her.

'Look,' Barbara said suddenly. 'There's Margaret. Out of bed again, and showing us more of her lovely new clothes.'

'Hello, Margaret,' Antonia called. 'Nice to see you. Come and walk with us.'

'It will be nicer when you two are less fat and ugly,' said Margaret pleasantly. She was wearing narrow red trousers on her long legs, and a warm red jacket. 'Come and play, Susie!'

Annoyed, Antonia watched as Susie ran laughing to Margaret, who took both the child's hands, and swung her round and round. Susie screamed with delight.

'You should have a child of your own,' Antonia said.

'Ugh! What a nasty idea,' said Margaret. 'If I had a child, I would drown it immediately.'

Barbara laughed, thinking, as she told James later, that Margaret was just trying, in her strange way, to be funny.

'Come on, Susie, let's run,' Margaret shouted, and she chased the laughing child around the lake.

'It's good to see Margaret enjoying herself,' Barbara said. 'She seems so much better these days.'

'She's never been ill,' Antonia said. 'She's comfortable in bed and doesn't have to work. She's just lazy and selfish. But she does have a lovely figure.'

'Yes. Oh! Should they go so near the edge of the lake?'

'No! Oh, be careful! Stop!' Antonia screamed as Margaret,

swinging Susie round and round, slipped on the icy ground and let go of Susie, who flew away from her and landed with a splash in the lake.

Antonia and Barbara threw themselves into the water.

'Her hands slipped out of mine,' said Margaret, standing on the path.

Barbara and Antonia, waist deep in the lake, lifted Susie out of the water and held her, silent and white-faced in shock, between them.

'You were stupid not to take your boots off,' said Margaret.

Susie, taking a deep breath, began to scream.

'Oh well, I can see she's all right,' Margaret said.

Henry, crossing the field with his dogs, had seen the three women and realized something was wrong. He began to run.

When he arrived, he saw that neither of the pregnant women could move easily. He reached out and took Susie from them, then went into the lake and pulled both women out. His face was white with anger and fear.

'It was an accident,' Barbara said.

'She tried to drown her.' Antonia's voice shook with cold. 'She's a murderer. Look, she's walking away.'

'We've lost our boots in the lake,' Barbara said, and began to cry. Both women were blue with cold.

'My brave girls. Quick,' Henry said, kissing Antonia. 'Let's get you home. I don't want to lose my babies.'

'Yours—?' Barbara whispered, as Henry kissed her too, and he, with his mouth on hers, said, 'James's.'

Margaret slipped on the icy ground and let go of Susie.

'Hurry,' he said, 'or you will freeze. Come on, Susie, let's get you all warm and dry. Look, there's your dad and James.'

James and Matthew were running to meet them when Antonia's pains started.

'Ow, ow, ow!' she cried, and held on to Henry. 'You wanted to know,' she said to Barbara, 'what the pain is like. Ouch, ow, OW! It's like this!'

—◈—

'Pilar!' Margaret shouted as she went into the house, 'I am cold. I shall go to bed. Bring me some tea.'

Before Pilar reached the kitchen, Henry hurried in. 'Help us, Pilar!' he cried. 'Take Susie. She's been in the lake. I must telephone the doctor.'

Pilar took the child as Matthew and James led their wives into the house. Halfway up the stairs Margaret sat down to watch.

Henry was telephoning the doctor. 'He *can't* be out. Where is he? Where? What? Yes, it's an emergency!'

Trying to be calm, Matthew said, 'Tell him to be quick!'

In Pilar's arms, Susie screamed, 'Mummy, Mummy!'

'Aaah!' Antonia, bending over, cried out in pain.

Barbara said crossly to James, 'Make yourself useful! Go and get us some dry clothes!'

'What a noise!' Margaret said. 'Pilar! Where's my tea?'

'The doctor will be as quick as he can,' Henry said.

James ran down the stairs, carrying warm coats and blankets. Matthew took a blanket and put it round Antonia. As he did so, a man came into the hall.

'Thank God you're here, doctor!' Matthew said. 'It's my wife. Her baby shouldn't be born for another month yet.'

'I'm not a doctor.' The man stepped backwards in alarm. 'I came to see . . .'

'What are *you* doing here?' Margaret said from the stairs. 'I thought you were dead!'

'Not yet,' said the man. 'You look well. What's going on?'

'Something most unpleasant,' said Margaret. 'Perhaps *you* could get me some tea. I went out, and now I'm awfully cold.'

'I don't know where the tea is. I heard you lived in bed.'

'Who told you?'

'The people I'm staying with. The Jonathans.'

Matthew said, 'So you're not the doctor?'

'I'm afraid not.'

Margaret said, 'This is my brother Basil.'

Matthew turned back to Antonia, and saw Henry putting another blanket round her. Suddenly angry, he pushed Henry away. 'Let *me* do that,' he said.

From the stairs Margaret shouted, 'Where's my *tea*?'

'Good idea,' Henry said quietly, and left the room.

When the doctor arrived, he decided to move Antonia to the local hospital immediately. 'You must come too,' he told Barbara. 'I believe your baby is expected soon.'

'Well, actually, I think it's coming now,' Barbara told him, 'but I don't want to frighten my husband.'

The doctor laughed.

Henry stood by the door and watched them go.

Basil joined him at the door, planning to introduce himself, and arrange a quieter time to come back and talk to him.

———◇◇◇———

'Aren't our daughters lovely?' Antonia said to the Jonathans, who had come to the hospital to visit her and Barbara.

'Not as pretty as their mothers,' they said. 'And what about the dads? Is Matthew delighted?'

'If he is, he's hiding it well,' Antonia said. Matthew had two daughters now, but he did not have the son he wanted.

'Tell us about Basil,' Barbara said. 'What's he like?'

'He's a kind man, I think,' said John. 'Not like his sister.'

'Why have we never heard of him? What's the mystery?'

'There's no mystery,' said the Jonathans. 'Basil's a friend of a friend. He went to live in America, but he's in England on business, and thought he'd visit his sister. He hasn't done it before because they don't like each other, and never have.'

'But what happened,' said Barbara, 'when we went off to hospital? What did he and Henry say to each other? Tell us.'

Suddenly angry, Jonathan said, 'Very well, I shall. When you left, Basil decided to leave too, and come back another time. He found Henry on the doorstep, blinded by tears.'

Barbara said, 'Oh, my God,' and began to weep.

'What else did Basil tell you?' Antonia asked quietly.

'Nothing. He and Henry went for a long walk, and talked and talked. But Basil did not tell us what Henry talked about. He said it was private.'

—◇◇◇—

Margaret's brother Basil had had to run because Henry walked so fast. Finally, he stopped by the gate to a field. Basil saw that tears were still running down his face.

'It's so awful,' Henry said. 'When they first came here, they were just silly young girls. Now they are women having babies.' He paused. 'Are you really Margaret's brother?'

'Yes,' said Basil. 'But don't worry about it.'

'I won't,' said Henry, and began walking again.

'I haven't seen Margaret for a long time,' Basil said. Was Henry listening? he wondered. He went on talking anyway. 'She's always been lazy and selfish, and I was glad when she went to Egypt. Then she married that German. A stupid thing to do, because he was, well, like your friends, the Jonathans. And like me. So the marriage didn't last, but it meant she had a German passport, which was dangerous for her during the war. The Jonathans told me all this. We all know the rest, about your father's acts of kindness to women in danger. But this one, it seems, you had to do.'

Henry stared ahead miserably. 'I am not wanted at the hospital, I shall not go.'

'What?' said Basil. Then, 'But why did you marry her?'

'What business is it of yours?' said Henry rudely. 'Oh, you must forgive me, I'm so . . . It's Antonia and Barbara. I find it difficult to think of anyone else.'

'Those girls will be all right,' Basil said. 'I'm sure they will. But please tell me why you married Margaret. And why do you stay with her?'

'Strangely enough,' Henry said, 'the marriage gives me a kind of freedom. So the Jonathans told you about their part in my marriage. I've suspected it, but never been sure.'

'They say they were helping your father do one more act of kindness before he died. They thought he was wonderful, the way he tried to help people in danger because of the war.'

'It came at a bad time for me,' Henry said. 'And I expected

61

to get killed in the war, anyway. So I thought, Why not, and married your sister. But I wasn't killed, and I brought her to Cotteshaw and tried to make the marriage a success. I thought she would want the same, but she didn't. She went

Was Henry listening? Basil wondered. He went on talking anyway.

to bed, and there she stays. She gets up from time to time, but that isn't always a good thing – look at what happened today.'

'She seemed to enjoy herself,' Basil said.

'People try to help her,' Henry went on. 'Pilar and Trask are wonderful.' He paused and then said quietly, 'I once tried to sleep with her. I thought she might be happier if she had a child. That was stupid of me. She threw a knife at me.'

'My God,' Basil said. 'But how do you survive?'

'I manage. I have some women friends. I have my farm. The Jonathans work the vegetable gardens, and the two young families pay rent to use the house at weekends.' He began to walk faster, and Basil heard him whisper to himself, 'But now, I don't know . . . I must step back, keep away.'

'I don't understand,' said Basil. 'What's the problem?'

'Antonia and Barbara, of course. Their babies!' Henry shouted. 'I'm so worried about it all.'

'But why?' Basil said. He was now some way behind Henry. 'It seems to me,' he called, 'that you are jealous.'

Henry stopped. 'Jealous?' he said. 'Jealous?' There was surprise in his voice, but there was pain, too.

PART FIVE

8

Children and grandchildren

James Martineau and Matthew Stephenson, meeting at a garage in London one day, stood for a while chatting.

'How are the girls, and the grandchildren?' asked James.

Matthew's daughters Susie and Clio were both married. Susie had a son, Guy, and Clio had a little daughter, Katie.

'They're all fine,' said Matthew. 'Did we tell you that Guy is going to go to Eton?'

'I had heard,' said James. 'Are you pleased about it?'

'Well, Susie wants it,' Matthew said. 'I'm sorry now that I allowed Antonia's father to pay for Susie to go to a private school. It was a mistake. Susie's grown up to be rather bossy. Now she wants the best school in the country for Guy, and she expects me to pay. I'd prefer my grandchildren to have the life that Clio and Hilaria had as children. They went to ordinary schools and had all those wonderful weekends and holidays at Cotteshaw.'

'Times have changed,' James said. 'Pilar is back in Spain. Trask is dead, and Henry has grown old and ill. Cotteshaw isn't the same as when we were young.'

'True,' Matthew said, 'but how our children loved it. And Clio's girl Katie loves Cotteshaw, too. She'd rather go there than have exciting foreign holidays.'

James laughed. 'It's the same with our granddaughter. Hilaria takes Eliza down to Cotteshaw as often as Clio takes Katie, I should think. But it can't last for ever.'

'Well, I must get on,' said Matthew. 'Let's meet soon.'

James drove away, thinking about Matthew. How old he looks, he thought. I look better at sixty-five than he does. Then he remembered the good times at Cotteshaw. What fun the children had when they were small – running wild on the farm, Henry teaching them to ride and swim.

I've had a happy life, he thought. I may not be as rich or successful as Matthew, but I have a wonderful wife, and a lovely daughter and granddaughter. How awful to have a daughter like Susie, so rude and bossy! I'm not surprised that Clio gets on better with our Hilaria than with her own sister.

Matthew, driving away in his more expensive car, thought about James. He felt rather sorry for his old friend. He's not done as well as I have, he thought. And he has no son or grandson. I wonder if he is jealous of me?

Matthew also thought about Cotteshaw. It was true, he thought, things were different now. With Pilar gone and Trask dead, Henry was on his own, except when Clio and Hilaria visited. But in the old days Cotteshaw had been home to both families. Growing up, the little girls had run round the farm behind Henry or Trask, watched Pilar cook, sat on Henry's knee while he read stories to them. Sometimes the children's love for Henry had been a bit annoying. But also useful. Henry had often, helped by Pilar, taken care of the children while their parents had enjoyed holidays together.

And it had all ended because of poor bossy Susie, Matthew thought. She wanted to make Margaret's life better, but instead of that she destroyed our happy times at Cotteshaw.

—◇◇◇—

It had happened in the summer of 1970. Susie was fourteen. She'd had a fight with her sister Clio and Hilaria, and she was bored and cross. Wanting something different to do, she asked Trask if she could take Margaret's lunch to her. Trask was tired and his legs hurt. He was glad to let Susie help.

Susie walked into Margaret's room, which was now blue. She felt rather nervous of the beautiful woman in the bed, but Margaret looked at her and said, 'You're much too pretty to be Antonia's daughter. Sit down!' Soon, she was showing Susie her dresses, and telling her about her first husband, her life in Egypt, and her marriage to Henry.

Susie began to feel that Margaret's strange behaviour was all Henry's fault. She saw herself as the one person who could save Margaret and give her a happier life. She would persuade Margaret to leave her bed.

Margaret began to take walks in the garden with Susie. It was a hot summer, and Clio and Hilaria were spending all their time by the lake, jumping in and out of the water. Susie wanted to swim, too, but she would not go to the lake without Margaret. At supper one evening, she told everyone, 'I'm going to teach Margaret to swim.'

'Please don't, Susie,' said Henry. 'You don't understand Margaret.'

'I understand Margaret very well,' Susie said, in her

annoying way. 'She's a different person when she's with me.'

Henry shouted at her then, and the girls laughed. This made Susie angry, and she decided to teach Margaret to swim the next day. Both lots of parents were away, so there was no one except Henry to prevent Susie from doing this.

In the morning, Clio and Hilaria were jumping in and out of the water, as usual. Susie led Margaret through the garden, and put a blanket on the grass by the lake for her to sit on.

'Shall we swim?' she asked after a while.

'You swim,' Margaret said. 'I'll watch you.'

Susie showed Margaret everything Henry had taught her, swimming on her front and on her back and under the water. 'It's lovely!' she shouted. 'Come on in, Margaret. I'll show you what to do. If you feel nervous, I'll help you.'

—◆◇◆—

'We didn't see her go in. We were getting dressed.'

'My head was covered by my T-shirt.'

Hilaria and Clio wept and wept; they had been too frightened to scream.

Henry was out of breath when he reached the lake, and Margaret, panicking, had pulled Susie down under the water. When Henry got them out, Susie was unconscious and Margaret was dead.

All this Matthew remembered as he drove away from the garage after meeting James that day in 1990.

—◆◇◆—

Later that same year Antonia and Barbara drove down from London to Cotteshaw in Antonia's car.

'What's the latest news?' Antonia asked. 'Is Henry better or worse?'

'Worse. It always gets worse with emphysema. It's slow at the beginning, but he's had it for years now.'

'Poor Henry. Sad to see him like this.'

'Yes,' said Barbara. 'He's a lovely man.'

After a pause, Antonia said, 'Did you ever sleep with him?'

'Sleep with Henry?' said Barbara. 'No! Why, did you?'

'Yes,' Antonia said. 'I slept with him from time to time. It was most enjoyable. Are you sure you didn't?'

'Of course I didn't sleep with Henry!'

She did, Antonia thought, I know she did. And to think that at one time we used to tell each other everything.

Barbara said, 'Antonia, you know he's dying.'

'Yes. I shall miss him more than I can say. Should we stay at the house tonight? I've brought my things.'

'No. Don't be hurt, but I don't think Clio and Hilaria want us to stay.'

'I'm not hurt. Henry has always belonged more to them than to us. They were almost born at Cotteshaw, remember, and they saw him save Susie.'

Barbara said, 'I knew he was dying when he decided not to get any more dogs when the old ones died.'

'Oh, Barbara, don't cry,' said Antonia. 'Then I'll start crying, and drive us off the road.'

'Henry was so wonderful and comforting when I was unhappy!' wept Barbara.

When was that? wondered Antonia. I don't remember a

time like that. 'We're almost there,' she said. 'Look! There's Hilaria with Eliza.'

Barbara hugged her daughter and granddaughter, and Hilaria led them upstairs. 'Henry hasn't been downstairs for weeks,' she said. 'He gets tired so easily now.'

Henry lay in bed, and the two women were shocked to see how thin and weak he was. But his eyes shone at the sight of them, and he said, 'Hello girls!'

Clio was sitting by the window, and a child similar to but

'Hello, girls!' Henry said.

69

smaller than Eliza was lying at Henry's feet. Henry said, 'These little girls have taken the place of my dogs.'

Clio took Katie downstairs, so that Barbara and Antonia could be alone with Henry. His breathing was noisy and painful to hear.

'The little girls are so sweet,' he told their grandmothers. 'They sing and dance for me.'

From his bed he could look out across the garden to his fields and woods. Birds were singing. I wish I could go out there, he thought. I wish they would not listen to my breathing. Soon he was tired. 'Ask the girls to come back,' he whispered. 'I need a drink.'

'But we can bring you a drink, Henry.'

'They know what I like,' he whispered, and Barbara and Antonia knew that he wanted them to leave. Clio and Hilaria, Eliza and Katie, were taking care of everything.

'They are pushing us out,' Antonia said sadly, as they drove back to London.

There were other visitors. Pilar came from Spain. She told Henry she had read his father's letter all those years ago. Opened it, read it, then posted it.

'I did wrong,' she said, 'but your father wanted it, and he saved me and Ebro. How could I refuse an old man's last wish? But I know now an old man's last wish is often stupid.'

Henry laughed, then had to fight to get his breath. When he could speak, he said, 'Dear Pilar, you did right.'

The Jonathans came often, and read to him. They were older than Henry, and their own health was not good. Clio thought that they came too often, and made Henry too tired, but Hilaria said they were part of Henry's life and he wanted them there.

One afternoon, Calypso came, bringing flowers. She was alone, as Hector had died many years before.

'How are you?' she asked.

'Dying,' Henry said. 'It's slow work.'

'Hector died so suddenly,' Calypso said. 'There was no chance to talk. What is it like?'

'Exhausting. I can't breathe, and I'm not allowed to laugh.'

'Clio and Hilaria told me not to make you laugh.'

Henry said, 'When I can't sleep at night, I think about the times when Barbara and James and Antonia and Matthew came here with their babies. They were happy times. And now Clio and Hilaria are taking care of me.'

'They love you,' Calypso said, 'and their husbands can manage without them for a while.'

'Hilaria isn't actually married to her child's father.'

'That's the new way. It's very fashionable.'

'Not as new as you think!'

'Don't laugh,' Calypso said. 'I'll be in trouble with Clio.'

'Should I tell you my secrets, now I am dying?' he asked.

'No!' Calypso said quickly. 'You have lived a good and brave life. Don't start wishing now that it had been different.'

Henry said, 'I think you know all my secrets, anyway.'

'That's possible,' Calypso said.

Clio, coming upstairs, was surprised to hear laughter.

———◇◇◇———

It was hard, waiting for Henry to die. Clio and Hilaria sat with him while the little girls played outside and the Jonathans stayed downstairs to answer the telephone.

'No change,' they said to callers. 'Perhaps a little weaker. He sleeps most of the time. Yes, we'll give him your love.'

One day Susie phoned. When he put down the phone, John said, 'I shall explode if Henry has left Cotteshaw to her.'

'Don't be silly,' Jonathan told him. 'I'm sure that Katie and Eliza will have Cotteshaw.'

The two old men sat side by side, staring sadly out into the garden. It began to rain, and Jonathan said, 'The little girls will have to come in. What shall we do with them?'

'Let's show them the old photographs,' said John. 'They'll love that.'

He was right. The children sat on the floor, surrounded by books of photos, saying, 'Oh, what funny clothes!' and 'Tell me, who is this?' while it grew dark outside, and the old men enjoyed a glass of whisky.

They looked at photographs of Pilar as a young woman and Ebro as a baby, Henry as a young man with his dogs, and Henry's strange, beautiful wife, Margaret. Then they found their mothers and grandparents and themselves as babies.

John was half asleep in his chair when the girls began arguing over a photo of a young woman. Each was shouting, 'It's *my* mother, not hers! Tell her, John! It's *my* mother!'

72

He took the photograph and looked at it. 'This was taken in 1930,' he said, 'long before your mothers were born. This is Henry's mother.' Then, as his eyes met Jonathan's over the children's heads, he said, 'Of course, there's a look . . .'

In the early hours of the morning, the rain stopped. Henry woke up and tried to speak. 'Air,' he whispered. Clio opened the window wide.

The children had come in during the night, and were asleep in chairs. 'Don't wake them,' he whispered.

Clio and Hilaria held his hands as they grew colder.

'Is it light?' he asked.

'Nearly.'

A bird began to sing in the garden, but Henry Tillotson had died a moment before.

73

GLOSSARY

act something that somebody does (e.g. a kind act, a selfish act)
Bentley a large and expensive type of English car
boredom the experience of being bored
bossy always telling people what to do
candle a stick of wax which is burnt to give light
cart a vehicle with two wheels, pulled by a horse, and used for
  carrying things or people
chat *(v)* to talk in a friendly way about unimportant things
cheerful happy and smiling
cockatoo a kind of parrot
Dior Christian Dior, a famous French dress designer who made
  beautiful clothes for rich women
divorce *(v)* to end a marriage, using the law
emphysema a serious illness, which makes it difficult to breathe
engaged having promised to marry someone
Eton a very famous and expensive English school for boys
forgive to stop feeling angry with someone who has done
  something to harm or annoy you
godfather a man chosen by the parents of a new baby to take a
  special interest in the child as he or she grows up
guest a person that you have invited to your house (for a meal, a
  party, a visit, etc.)
horrible very unpleasant, nasty
hug *(v)* to put your arms around someone and hold them, to
  show that you like or love them
landlord a man who owns or manages a pub
make love (to/with someone) to have sex with someone
nervous afraid, worried

ordinary normal, not unusual or special in any way
panic (past tense **panicked**) to lose control because of fear, so
  that you cannot think clearly or behave sensibly
perfume a sweet-smelling liquid which you put on your body
pregnant expecting a baby
quarrel *(v)* to have an angry argument or disagreement
queer *(n)* an offensive, slang word for a homosexual (a man
  who loves other men)
redecorate to put new paint or paper on the walls of a room
refugee someone who has to leave their own country (usually
  because of a war) and start life again in another country
rent *(v & n)* to pay money to use something (e.g. a house or a
  car) which someone else owns
sex a physical relationship between two people
shabby in poor condition, needing repairs
share *(v & n)* to let somebody use something that is yours
shock *(n)* an unpleasant surprise
sleep with (**somebody**) to have sex with somebody
slip *(v)* to fall or nearly fall when your foot accidentally slides
  on something wet, icy, etc.; to slide out of your hand
strawberry a soft red fruit
swing (past tense **swung**) to hold something/body and move it/
  them through the air from side to side, round and round, etc.
thoughtful showing you think about and care for other people
weep (past tense **wept**) to cry, usually because you are sad

ACTIVITIES

Before Reading

1 Read the story introduction on the first page of the book, and the back cover. Can you guess what will happen in the story? Choose answers to these questions (as many as you like).

1 Who will be divorced by the end of the story?
   a) Barbara and her husband   c) Henry and Margaret
   b) Antonia and her husband   d) Nobody

2 Why does Margaret stay in bed all the time? Because . . .
   a) she is ill.   c) she is mad.
   b) she wants to be difficult.   d) she is lazy.

3 Why is Henry so forgiving? Because . . .
   a) he is a kind man.   c) he likes a quiet life.
   b) he loves his wife.   d) he feels sorry for his wife.

2 Use a dictionary to find out the meanings of 'dubious' and 'legacy'. Then choose answers to these questions.

1 What can 'dubious' mean? (Choose two answers.)
   a) feeling doubtful or uncertain about something
   b) not understanding the meaning of something
   c) probably not honest, or of doubtful truth

2 What can 'legacy' mean? (Choose two answers.)
   a) something left to you by another person when they die
   b) a situation that is the result of what happened in the past
   c) something that is yours to use only until you die

While Reading

Read Part 1, Chapter 1, and then answer these questions.

1 What annoyed Margaret about her arrival at the station?
2 What did Margaret do when she arrived at Cotteshaw?
3 What did Henry ask the two Jonathans to do when he left?
4 After Henry left, Jonathan said, 'It's gone wrong this time, hasn't it?' What do you think he was talking about?
5 What was the terrible trap that Henry found himself in?

Read Part 2, Chapters 2 to 5. Are these sentences true (T)   or false (F)? Rewrite the false ones with the correct information.

1 At their first meeting Margaret told Antonia and Barbara a great many lies about Henry.
2 Antonia and Barbara both preferred to have an exciting husband and a perfect married life.
3 Pilar wished now that she had not posted the letter Henry's father had written to Henry during the war.
4 Henry gave Barbara and Antonia a Dior dress.
5 In Egypt in the war, when Calypso refused to marry Henry, he decided to do what his father had asked.
6 The dinner party was a great success.
7 Henry blamed himself for the way Margaret behaved.
8 By the end of the evening, both girls had quarrelled with their future husbands.

Before you read Part 3, Chapter 6 (*Barbara's problem and Antonia's boredom*), try to guess answers to these questions.

1 What is Barbara's problem?

   a) She can't have a child.   c) She doesn't love James.

   b) She hates Margaret.   d) She's in love with Matthew.

2 What is the answer to Antonia's boredom?

   a) She gets a job.   c) She leaves her husband.

   b) She takes a lover.   d) She moves to Cotteshaw.

Read Part 3, Chapter 6. Choose the best question-word for these questions, and then answer them.

What / Why / How

1 . . . had changed at Cotteshaw between 1954 and 1958?

2 . . . was making Barbara unhappy when Henry visited her?

3 . . . did Barbara do when James came home and apologized?

4 . . . did Antonia go to visit Margaret?

5 . . . three different things made Antonia angry on the night that she went to Hector and Calypso's?

6 . . . did Antonia do with the advice that her mother gave her?

7 . . . did Antonia decide to tell her secret to Calypso?

8 . . . did Henry save Antonia's marriage?

9 . . . did Antonia and Calypso disagree about Henry's life?

10 . . . do you think Antonia meant when she said to Calypso, 'It's good for Henry, with no children of his own, to have a share in ours'?

Read Part 4, Chapter 7. Who said this, and to whom? Who, or what, were they talking about?

1 'It's awful! Terrible!'
2 'You forget all about it when it's over.'
3 'Ugh! What a nasty idea.'
4 'She tried to drown her. She's a murderer.'
5 'I think it's coming now, but I don't want to frighten my husband.'
6 'He hasn't done it before because they don't like each other, and never have.'
7 'But this one, it seems, you had to do.'
8 'I've suspected it, but never been sure.'
9 'I must step back, keep away.'

Before reading Part 5, Chapter 8, can you guess the answers to these questions? Choose as many names as you like.

1 Who causes a terrible accident at Cotteshaw in 1970?
   Barbara / Clio / Susie / Margaret / Hilaria / Antonia
2 By the end of the story in 1990, who has died?
   Henry / Trask / Margaret / Calypso / Hector / James / Matthew / Barbara / Antonia / Susie / nobody
3 By the end of the story in 1990, who knows for sure who Clio's and Hilaria's real father is? Who probably suspects who it is?
   James / Matthew / Susie / the Jonathans / Margaret / Pilar / Calypso / nobody

ACTIVITIES

After Reading

1 **Here is the letter that Henry's father wrote to Henry in Egypt during the war. Complete the letter by choosing the best word for each gap.**

I am dying, my _____, and the dearest wish _____ my heart is that _____ help a young woman _____ is in great danger _____ Cairo. Margaret Gottschalk is _____, but because her divorced _____ was German, she now _____ only a German passport. _____ of this, the British _____ probably put her in _____, although she has done _____ wrong. To get a _____ passport, she needs a _____ husband. Will you marry _____ and save her from _____? You will make me _____ happy if you do. _____ have always been a _____ son – and I am _____ you will be a _____ husband as well.

Your _____ father

2 **Complete this conversation between Barbara and Antonia after Margaret's death. Use as many words as you like.**

ANTONIA: Oh Barbara, there's been a terrible accident at Cotteshaw. Margaret's dead.

BARBARA: Dead?! Oh no! How did it happen?

ANTONIA: She and Susie _____

BARBARA: But Margaret can't swim!

ANTONIA: _____

80

BARBARA: Oh, poor Susie! Did anyone see them go under?
ANTONIA: _____

BARBARA: My God, how awful! Is Susie all right now?
ANTONIA: _____

BARBARA: But she mustn't blame herself. It was an accident.
And we all know what Margaret was like.
ANTONIA: _____

BARBARA: Yes, very different. I can't really imagine
Cotteshaw without Margaret. Poor old Henry . . .

3 There are many secrets in this story, but who do you think knew
which ones? Make as many sentences as you can with these
names, about the secrets in this table.

James / Matthew / the Jonathans / Calypso / Margaret /
Antonia / Barbara

	certainly probably perhaps never	knew didn't know	who Clio's father was. who Hilaria's father was. who Henry loved. who first suggested Henry should marry Margaret.
_____			

Now explain why you think this, by adding to your sentences any
explanations or ideas that you can find in the story.

Example: Calypso probably knew who Clio's father was
because Antonia told her about sleeping with Henry, and
Calypso had seen herself how fond Henry was of the little girls.

81

4 Here is Henry, thinking about the women in his life at different times in the story. Who is he thinking about, and what has just happened in the story at that moment?

1 'Oh dear. That was a big mistake. Why ever did I think it was a good idea for her to join us? And that poor bird! I suppose I'd better take her up to her room now.'

2 'Dear girls – nice of them to come. Still so pretty. Hard to believe they're grandmothers. But they don't know me like the little girls do. So tired. Always so tired now . . .'

3 'There they go. I do hope they're going to be all right – and the babies. Oh, I wish, I wish – but I can't, I'm not wanted. I mustn't cry . . . oh no . . . got to get away from here . . .'

4 'Ow! That really hurt! I could see she wasn't pleased about the car, but I didn't think she was as angry as that! Not a good start. Let's hope she calms down a bit now . . .'

5 'Poor girl. James should take more care of her. Still, I think she's happier now than she was this morning. I certainly am! If they knew about this down at Cotteshaw . . .!'

6 'That's just like her! Asking me what it feels like to be dying! No, mustn't laugh . . . I wonder if she really does know all my secrets? I wouldn't be at all surprised . . .'

7 'Mmm. Lovely brown hair. And the other one's nice-looking too. Well done, Matthew and James – you've got a couple of nice girls there. I wonder which one – no, mustn't think about that. Time to say hello to the boys.'

5 Here are some of the things the characters say about marriage. Who says each one? What does it tell us about them? Have their ideas changed by the end of the story?

1 'We decided a long time ago to find husbands who can take good care of us.'

2 'With (. . .) it will be different. She's young and inexperienced, and I will be the boss.'

3 'I really need a wife, to do business dinners for me.'

4 'You will never be free of me, and you will never have children. I shall make certain of that.'

5 'I can't divorce her. Who would take care of her if I did?'

6 'I wasn't in love with him when I married him, but I am now. I want to make him happy, but I just disappoint him.'

7 'After we'd made love, I decided I would never leave (. . .) and I would make a success of my marriage.'

8 'Strangely enough, the marriage gives me a kind of freedom.'

6 What do you think the 'dubious legacy' of the title means, and is *A Dubious Legacy* a good title for this story? Why, or why not? What do you think of the titles below? Explain why you think they would make better, or worse, titles for the story.

Henry's Daughters   The Many Names of Love
A Father's Wish   The Lovers of Cotteshaw
A Shared Life   Giving and Taking
Secrets and Lies   Queen of Cotteshaw
A Selfish Man   Like Father, Like Son

ABOUT THE AUTHOR

'People assume,' Mary Wesley once said, 'that I sat down at the age of seventy and started to write. This is quite untrue. I have been writing all my life for my own pleasure but invariably what I wrote I consigned to the rubbish-bin. Looking back, I understand that I was teaching myself to write.'

Mary Wesley's path to success as a novelist was an unusual one. She was born in Berkshire in 1912, and her father's job as an army officer meant frequent moves, so she had few friends as a child. In 1936 she married Lord Swinfen and they had two sons, but the marriage was unhappy and ended in the 1940s. Later she fell in love with the journalist Eric Siepmann and lived with him for several years before they married. Because of this her parents cut her out of their wills, and when Siepmann died in 1970 she had very little money.

Siepmann had encouraged her to write, however, and in 1983, when she was seventy-one, her first major novel was published. This was *Jumping the Queue*, which ends with a successful suicide. It became a bestseller, as did later novels, including *The Camomile Lawn*, which has also been adapted for television. Her stories reflect the upper-middle-class world that Wesley grew up in. Loveless marriage is a frequent theme, as in *A Dubious Legacy*, and there is often a rather shy young woman, surrounded by self-confident and independent women; this echoes Wesley's own experiences when young.

As well as novels, Wesley wrote *Part of the Scenery* (2001), a memoir of the west of England, where she spent much of her life. She died in 2002.

ABOUT BOOKWORMS

OXFORD BOOKWORMS LIBRARY
*Classics • True Stories • Fantasy & Horror • Human Interest
Crime & Mystery • Thriller & Adventure*

The OXFORD BOOKWORMS LIBRARY offers a wide range of original and adapted stories, both classic and modern, which take learners from elementary to advanced level through six carefully graded language stages:

Stage 1 (400 headwords)	**Stage 4** (1400 headwords)
Stage 2 (700 headwords)	**Stage 5** (1800 headwords)
Stage 3 (1000 headwords)	**Stage 6** (2500 headwords)

More than sixty titles are also available on cassette, and there are many titles at Stages 1 to 4 which are specially recommended for younger learners. In addition to the introductions and activities in each Bookworm, resource material includes photocopiable test worksheets and Teacher's Handbooks, which contain advice on running a class library and using cassettes, and the answers for the activities in the books.

Several other series are linked to the OXFORD BOOKWORMS LIBRARY. They range from highly illustrated readers for young learners, to playscripts, non-fiction readers, and unsimplified texts for advanced learners.

Oxford Bookworms Starters   *Oxford Bookworms Factfiles*
Oxford Bookworms Playscripts   *Oxford Bookworms Collection*

Details of these series and a full list of all titles in the OXFORD BOOKWORMS LIBRARY can be found in *Oxford English* catalogues and also on our website www.oup.com/elt. A selection of titles from the OXFORD BOOKWORMS LIBRARY can be found on the next pages.

BOOKWORMS · HUMAN INTEREST · STAGE 4

Little Women

LOUISA MAY ALCOTT

Retold by John Escott

When Christmas comes for the four March girls, there is no money for expensive presents and they give away their Christmas breakfast to a poor family. But there are no happier girls in America than Meg, Jo, Beth, and Amy. They miss their father, of course, who is away at the Civil War, but they try hard to be good so that he will be proud of his 'little women' when he comes home.

This heart-warming story of family life has been popular for more than a hundred years.

BOOKWORMS · THRILLER & ADVENTURE · STAGE 4

The Moonspinners

MARY STEWART

Retold by Diane Mowat

When Nicola arrives in Crete a day early, she gets more than just an extra day of holiday. She comes to a village where no one can be trusted, and she becomes involved in a murder mystery that puts her own life in danger.

This story is set in a small village in the mountains of Crete. This is an island where people have strong feelings, where arguments begin suddenly, and end quickly. And Nicola has arrived in the middle of an argument that could end very quickly – with a gun.

BOOKWORMS · CLASSICS · STAGE 4
A Tale of Two Cities

CHARLES DICKENS

Retold by Ralph Mowat

'The Marquis lay there, like stone, with a knife pushed into his heart. On his chest lay a piece of paper, with the words: *Drive him fast to his grave. This is from JACQUES.*'

The French Revolution brings terror and death to many people. But even in these troubled times people can still love and be kind. They can be generous and true-hearted . . . and brave.

Lord Jim

JOSEPH CONRAD

Retold by Clare West

A hundred years ago a seaman's life was full of danger, but Jim, the first mate on board the *Patna*, is not afraid of danger. He is young, strong, confident of his bravery. He dreams of great adventures – and the chance to show the world what a hero he is.

But the sea is no place for dreamers. When the chance comes, on a calm moonlit night in the Indian Ocean, Jim fails the test, and his world falls to pieces around him. He disappears into the jungles of south-east Asia, searching for a way to prove himself, once and for all . . .

BOOKWORMS · CLASSICS · STAGE 4

The Scarlet Letter

NATHANIEL HAWTHORNE

Retold by John Escott

Scarlet is the colour of sin, and the letter 'A' stands for 'Adultery'. In the 1600s, in Boston, Massachusetts, love was allowed only between a husband and a wife. A child born outside marriage was a child of sin.

Hester Prynne must wear the scarlet letter on her dress for the rest of her life. How can she ever escape from this public shame? What will happen to her child, growing up in the shadow of the scarlet letter? The future holds no joy for Hester Prynne.

And what will happen to her sinful lover – the father of her child?

BOOKWORMS · CLASSICS · STAGE 5

Sense and Sensibility

JANE AUSTEN

Retold by Clare West

Sometimes the Dashwood girls do not seem like sisters. Elinor is all calmness and reason, and can be relied upon for practical, common sense opinions. Marianne, on the other hand, is all sensibility, full of passionate and romantic feeling. She has no time for dull common sense – or for middle-aged men of thirty-five, long past the age of marriage.

True love can only be felt by the young, of course. And if your heart is broken at the age of seventeen, how can you ever expect to recover from the passionate misery that fills your life, waking and sleeping?